ROBERT B. DOWNS

LIBRARY OF CONGRESS
WASHINGTON
1985

The Center for the Book
Viewpoint Series
No. 14

Library of Congress Cataloging-in-Publication Data

Downs, Robert Bingham, 1903–
Books in my life.

(The Center for the Book viewpoint series ; no. 14)
1. Books and reading—Addresses, essays, lectures.
I. Title. II. Series: Center for the Book viewpoint
series ; 14.
Z1003.D743 1985   028′.9   85–600194
ISBN 0–8444–0509–4

The paper used in this publication meets
the requirements for permanence established by
the American National Standard for Information Sciences
"Permanence of Paper for Printed Library Materials,"
ANSI Z39.48-1984.

"Books Make a Difference" is a reading promotion theme of the Center for the Book in the Library of Congress. In 1980–81, under the sponsorship of the Center for the Book, journalists Gordon and Patricia Sabine of Virginia Polytechnic Institute and State University in Blacksburg, Virginia, traveled throughout the country and asked more than fourteen hundred Americans two questions: What book made a difference in your life and what was that difference? In their *Books That Made the Difference: What People Told Us* (The Shoe String Press, 1983), the Sabines reported that the books of Horatio Alger had been named by the well-known librarian Robert B. Downs. Because Mr. Downs's long and successful career has been devoted to demonstrating the power and vitality of books, particularly through best-selling works such as *Books That Changed the World* (1st ed., 1956; 2d ed., 1978), I found his answer revealing and wanted to know more about the books that had helped shape his life. Thus I asked Mr. Downs, a member of the Center for the Book's National Advisory Board, if he would provide more details. This essay is the result, and it is a pleasure to share it with a wider audience through its publication in the Center for the Book's Viewpoint Series.

Robert B. Downs is one of America's most distinguished academic librarians. He served as director of libraries at the University of North Carolina and New York University before becoming Dean of Library Administration at the University of Illinois, an office he held for twenty-eight years. He also is one of librarianship's most prolific authors. His writings include over two dozen books and 350 articles and reports. Seven major books may be considered part of his series aimed at convincing people that books are significant, that they have shaped civilization, and that they should be seen as important parts of our culture. They are:

Books That Changed the World (1956, 1978), *Molders of the Modern Mind* (1961), *Famous Books, Ancient and Medieval* (1964), *Books That Changed America* (1970), *Famous American Books* (1971), *Books That Changed the South* (1977), and *In Search of New Horizons: Epic Tales of Travel and Exploration* (1978).

Robert B. Downs's remarkable career in administration, education, and scholarship has been recognized by his peers through six honorary doctorates and many awards and citations. When he received the American Library Association's Clarence Day Award in 1963, the association, citing his writings about famous books, made a statement that is still true: "No librarian has reached such a wide audience and no librarian has made a richer contribution to an understanding of books for their enjoyment and for their significance for our time."

The Center for the Book in the Library of Congress was established by law in 1977 to focus national attention on the importance of books, reading, and the written word. An informal, voluntary organization funded primarily by private contributions, it brings together members of the book, educational, and business communities for projects and symposia. Drawing on the collections of the Library of Congress, it also sponsors publications, exhibitions, and events that enhance books and reading in our society.

JOHN Y. COLE
Executive Director
The Center for the Book

MY DEEP DEVOTION TO THE printed word began early. My father, a farmer-teacher and man of many talents, possessed a modest home library. Among my favorites from which I could select were *Robinson Crusoe*, *Gulliver's Travels*, *Treasure Island*, *From the Earth to the Moon*, *Tom Sawyer*, and the short stories of Poe and Bulwer-Lytton. *Alice's Adventures in Wonderland* and *Little Women* thoroughly bored me.

A fortunate circumstance supplemented the rather limited home resources. Once each year, the nearby one-room school, Shady Grove, held a box supper (the girls bringing boxes to be auctioned off to the highest bidders), and the proceeds were used to buy books for the school. During the long summer vacation, to avoid theft or vandalism, the books were stored in my home. In that way, I had ready access to a wealth of books for boys: those by Horatio Alger and by George A. Henty, the Rover Boys series, and others.

One of the first books to make a strong impression on me and to remain in my memory was *Aesop's Fables*, a copy of which I won for prowess in spelling, when about age ten. The fables have the merit of being easily understood by persons of any age, as they have been since the days of ancient Greece. Typically, of course, they are brief, simple, and direct—the language clear and unpretentious—incorporating folklore, tradition, superstition, and sophistry to teach a moral lesson. The pithy, didactic animal stories illustrate human foibles, while presenting common-sense moral principles. Frequently, I find myself reaching back to Aesop's tales to illustrate some important point, such as the fox and the grapes, the dog in the manger, the boy who cried wolf, and the goose that laid the golden eggs. Years later, I read the fables of Babrius, Phaedrus, and La Fontaine, but none of them held the fascination for me of Aesop.

Aesop's Fables is perhaps responsible for my longtime preoccupation with animal folklore, an area in which I have collected and occasionally published, for example, *The Bear Went Over the Mountain, Tall Tales of American Animals; American Humorous Folklore;* and *The Family Saga.* In fact animal tales have always held a special interest for me, starting with *Black Beauty,* the Brer Rabbit stories, *The Call of the Wild* and *White Fang,* Terhune's dog stories, *The Jungle Books,* the Tarzan yarns, and *Moby Dick.* Recently, I relived, with a feeling of nostalgia, the Tarzan story when I saw the motion picture *Greystoke.*

During elementary school and early high school, my reading fare was typical of popular boys' books of the time. My favorite authors, by all odds, were Horatio Alger and George A. Henty, both of whose prolific literary output I read by the yard. Alger's simplistic accounts of successful businessmen who, through honesty, tireless diligence, and unfailing loyalty, had progressed from poverty-stricken youth to wealth and eminence I found unfailingly inspiring and exciting. Alger, the most widely read author of juvenile books in the whole of American literature, indoctrinated millions of young Americans between the Civil War and World War I in the belief that virtue and hard work invariably bring financial rewards. Every immigrant landing on our shores, the poor farm boy remote from large cities, and the ragamuffin on the street were convinced by Alger that America was the land of opportunities. By pluck and luck, they could conquer poverty, defeat any villain, marry the boss's daughter, and live happily ever after.

What better evidence of these facts could be offered than the careers of certain leaders in the American business world? The post-Civil War era was the age of Rockefeller, Carnegie, Vanderbilt, Guggenheim, Harriman, Gould, Fisk, and other multimillionaires to whom great wealth came suddenly. Carnegie had risen from bobbin-boy to steel king, Buck (James B.) Duke from home-grown tobacco salesman on the road (including Yankee soldier customers behind the lines) to tobacco magnate, Thomas A. Edison from newsboy on Michigan trains to America's greatest inventor, James A. Farrell from laboring boy in a wire mill to president of U.S. Steel Corporation, Henry Ford from a twenty-five-dollar-a-week job polishing steam engines to head of the huge automotive corporation that still bears his name, Julius Rosenwald from door-to-door chromo salesman to president of Sears, Roebuck, and George Eastman from a three-dollar-a-week job in an insurance office to the founder of the Eastman Kodak Company. It could hardly be claimed, of course, that during their ascent they all strictly adhered to the elevated code of ethics constantly reiterated by Alger and his heroes.

In a different category was the influence on me, and on American and British boyhood generally, of George A. Henty, Alger's contemporary, with his extended series of books demonstrating Anglo-Saxon superiority in all eras of history. Henty brought a solid background of experience to his career as a novelist. Before writing some eighty books of adventure for boys, he had been a war correspondent during the Austro-Prussian War of 1866, had reported the Franco-Prussian War, had been in Asiatic Russia, and had seen action in a number of other military conflicts. His expert knowledge of military history lent verisimilitude to his books, each of which featured a boy hero, from ancient Egypt to the American Civil War and later.

From reading Henty's dramatic and memorable stories, I developed a lifelong devotion to history and biography, leading me to choose that field for my undergraduate major in college. My thinking was also influenced by reading such works as H.G. Wells's *Outline of History* and Alexis de Tocqueville's *Democracy in America.* Later, I put this avid interest to use in the preparation of works showing the impact of books on history and culture, *Books That Changed the World, Books That Changed America, Books That Changed the South,* and others.

For the dedicated bibliophile, a life surrounded by books comes near being idyllic. That has been my goal, from early years spent in the one-room schoolhouse with a few hundred volumes in the Blue Ridge Mountains of North Carolina until today, eight decades later. The horizon has constantly expanded to encompass the millions of volumes in such institutions as the New York Public Library, Columbia University, the University of North Carolina, and the University of Illinois.

My first step toward a wider view of the book world came at age fifteen, when my family moved from the farm to Asheville, where I was quickly exposed to the resources of an excellent public library, Pack Memorial. My rate of consumption was about a book a day. I was a high-school dropout for two years at the time, working at a variety of jobs, and had plenty of spare time for reading. Doubtless the books compensated to some extent for my lack of formal education during that period, but my reading was chiefly recreational, Zane Grey and the like.

Among American authors, Mark Twain has long occupied first place in my affection and estimation. Early on, I enjoyed his *Adventures of Tom Sawyer, Adventures of Huckleberry Finn,* and *Life on the Mississippi.* Recent attempts to ban *Huckleberry Finn* from libraries and classrooms on charges of racism seem to me to be completely misguided, and if successful would deprive American children of a superb literary masterpiece, rated by many critics as "the great American novel." Jim, the runaway slave who taught Huck something about the dignity and worth of a human life, is one of the most admirable characters in all American literature. An unforgettable experience for me was a visit to Mark Twain's Victorian-style home in Hartford, Connecticut. A complete set of his writings occupies a prominent place on my bookshelves.

Greater opportunities to become acquainted with the book world awaited me in Chapel Hill, when I entered the University of North Carolina's freshman class in 1922. Within a short time, I found employment as a student assistant in the library, with a chance to gain experience in nearly every department.

The UNC library was then under the direction of Louis Round Wilson, one of America's most famous librarians. His distinguished career has been summarized and evaluated in the new ALA publication *Leaders in American Academic Librarianship, 1925–1975,* edited by Wayne A. Wiegand, and earlier in Maurice Tauber's *Louis Round Wilson, Librarian and Administrator.* Those who knew him well stated that Wilson was never an avid reader but was primarily concerned with developing great book collections and suitable buildings to house them. Wilson had a remarkable gift for drawing upon and adapting the ideas of his associates. My decision to enter the library profession was directly influenced by Wilson, who advised me to enter the newly established School of Library Service at Columbia University in 1926.

Following my return to Chapel Hill in 1931 as assistant librarian and a member of the new library school faculty, I became concerned with books from the viewpoint of an educator. Of the courses assigned to me, the one that held the greatest attraction (both then and later at the University of Illinois) was the history of books and libraries. I have always contended that a librarian unacquainted with this subject is illiterate. Aside from teaching, my first literary effort to spread the message was a study guide, *The Story of Books,* published in 1935. As university librarian after 1932, I gave high priority to building up the collection of early printed books and other materials useful for teaching the history of books. The library at Chapel Hill held a strong collection of incunabula. The writings of Douglas McMurtrie, John C. Oswald, and other historians of printing were helpful to me and my students.

Incidents along the way turned my interests increasingly toward examining the impact of books on history and civilization. I found totally unacceptable comments that books were losing their popularity, were being superseded by newer forms of communication, and were becoming obsolete—a point of view expressed by doomsayers for generations. The perfect response came to me while listening to a lecture by a noted physiologist, who spoke on "Horsefeathers in Physiology," exploding many popular myths about digestion and related matters. It struck me that misconceptions were equally prevalent in my own profession. Therefore, as president of the American Library Association, I prepared and delivered on several occasions a talk entitled "Some Current Delusions, or Horsefeathers in Librarianship." Several key paragraphs follow.

There is a popular impression that books are harmless, innocent, and ineffective objects, full of theory and of little significance for the practical man of affairs. This statement may sound like a straw man, easy to knock down. Nevertheless, it reflects the attitude of a considerable element of the population. The general argument is that books have a place in the schools, that they are all right for children, invalids, and club women, and for recreational purposes in passing idle moments. Otherwise, they are of slight consequence. Such a point of view is responsible for the willingness of some administrators and trustees to cut library book budgets, and to feel that it doesn't make too much difference if there is a failure to acquire as many books as the librarian recommends.

The question boils down to this: Are books particularly important? Do they really matter? My answer is: Books have been, and are, the most potent force in our entire culture and civilization. Bulwer-Lytton epitomized the idea well in his famous line, "The pen is mightier than the sword." As Joseph Wood Krutch wrote not long ago, "The printed word is still the most generally efficient and effective method of conveying thought or information ever invented by man, and over the largest of all fields a hundred words are often worth a thousand pictures."

History provides the best evidence in support of my contention that books are not necessarily inanimate, peaceful articles, belonging to the cloistered shades and academic quiet of monasteries, universities, and other retreats from the evil world. If we take a glance back through the past, we can see how at variance the popular misconception is with the actual facts. Let me cite some examples. Consider how the writings of Martin Luther helped to produce the Protestant Revolution; how much Tom Paine's book *Common Sense,* circulating widely through the American colonies, did in creating the American Revolution; the part played by Harriet Beecher Stowe's *Uncle Tom's Cabin* in bringing on the American Civil War; the inspiration and philosophy furnished by Karl Marx's *Das Kapital* for the Russian Communist Revolution and other revolutionary movements; and the role of Adolf Hitler's *Mein Kampf* as the bible of Nazi Germany. Numerous other instances could be mentioned, including Admiral Mahan's *The Influence of Sea Power Upon History,* which has deeply influenced naval strategy and the construction of large navies during the past fifty or sixty years; and Karl Haushofer's *Power and Earth,* which in recent times, with its theory of geopolitics, has been the inspiration for world conquest. In a different field and more constructively, there might be named Darwin's *Origin of Species,* with its tremendous impact on science. A less well-known case, but one which led to immense consequences, is that of the Mahatma Gandhi who as a young man in South Africa read Henry Thoreau's *On the Duty of Civil Disobedience,* and was thereby inspired for his later campaign in India, a campaign which ended in India gaining her independence from Britain.

Throughout history, whenever dictators and other tyrants have wanted to suppress opposition and to kill ideas, their first thought, almost invariably, has been to destroy the books, and frequently their authors. These despots have recognized the enormous power of books and were fully conscious of the explosive forces they contain. Of course, the influence of books has at times been evil rather than beneficent. They can be forces for bad as well as for good. My point here, however, is not to try to measure moral values, but to show that the product with which we as librarians are dealing is a dynamic, vital material, capable of changing the direction of history.

At this time, I began an extensive program of reading and research to determine what particular books had most clearly and directly influenced historical events. At a meeting with Victor Weybright, head of the publishing firm of New American Library, I discussed the possibility of developing a full-length book on the same theme. He encouraged me to proceed with a manuscript. There were consultations with a variety of scientists, social scientists, and other scholars and specialists. The final result was the publication in 1956 of *Books That Changed the World,* a paperback in the New American Library's Mentor series and a hardback issued by the American Library Association.

Of the numerous books I have produced during the past fifty years, this has remained the most enduring in popular interest. The Mentor edition has sold hundreds of thousands of copies, and hardback editions rank high among ALA bestsellers. There have been foreign translations in Arabic, Bengali, Chinese, Indonesian, Japanese (4 editions), Korean, Malay, Persian, Portuguese, Spanish, Swedish, Turkish, Urdu, and Vietnamese. The Arabic, Chinese, and Turkish editions were pirated. The Chinese translation, issued in Taiwan, was reported to have sold fifty thousand copies shortly after publication. A condensed version, entitled *The Power of Books,* was published by the Syracuse University Press in 1958. An article, "Sixteen Books That Changed the World," appeared in the *Rotarian* in 1960. A Miami firm, Wills and Sons, proposed to publish a series of new editions of great books using my essays from *Books That Changed the World* for introductions. Only one was actually published, Thomas Paine's *Common Sense,* in 1975. Apparently the project was dropped at that point as not being financially feasible.

The original edition of *Books That Changed the World* was limited to sixteen titles, ten classified as "The World of Man" and six as "The World of Science," ranging from the sixteenth to the twentieth centuries. The first group included works by Niccolò Machiavelli, Thomas Paine, Adam Smith, Thomas Malthus, Henry David Thoreau, Harriet Beecher Stowe, Karl Marx, Alfred T. Mahan, Halford J. Mackinder, and Adolf Hitler. The scientific titles were by Nicolaus Copernicus, William Harvey, Isaac Newton, Charles Darwin, Sigmund Freud, and Albert Einstein.

Obviously the roots of modern civilization precede the sixteenth century by thousands of years, and a true understanding of our own culture must be based upon knowledge of the ancient and medieval worlds; therefore, when it was proposed to issue a second edition of *Books That Changed the World,* the coverage was considerably expanded. The ALA second edition, published in 1978, added to "The World of Man" section the Bible, Homer, Aesop, Plato, Aristotle, the great Greek playwrights, St. Augustine, and St. Thomas Aquinas and to "The World of Science" Greek and Roman scientists and for later periods Andreas Vesalius, Edward Jenner, and Rachel Carson. The contents of a new Mentor edition, issued in 1983, were similarly revised.

My theme on the influence of books was exploited further in two books published by Barnes & Noble: *Famous Books Ancient and Medieval,* about 108 great books that have shaped modern civilization, and *Molders of the Modern Mind* (a title later changed to *Famous Books Since 1492),* discussing 111 books.

The influence of books was explored further in my *Books That Changed America,* published in hardback by Macmillan and in paperback in the New American Library's Mentor series. A shorter version under the same title was published by the University of Denver Library School. Twenty-five books that, in my estimation, had made a profound impact on the nation's history and culture were analyzed in detail.

A follow-up in the same field was my *Famous American Books,* published by McGraw-Hill in 1971. The fifty titles included ranged from Amerigo Vespucci in 1505 to Paul Ehrlich in 1968.

An editorial adviser for Barnes & Noble recommended, after the two B. & N. titles went out of print, that selected chapters from both books be republished by Littlefield, Adams in Totowa, New Jersey. This was done and a handsome paperback edition appeared in 1975, entitled *Famous Books, Great Writings in the History of Civilization.* The sixty works included began with ancient Egypt's *Book of the Dead* and ended with Sigmund Freud's *Civilization and Its Discontents.*

It occurred to me that my native South would be a fertile field for a study of books that had made the greatest impact on the region. The director of the University of North Carolina Press, Matthew Hodgson, approved the idea. During the 1976 spring semester spent in Chapel Hill as a visiting faculty member in the School of Library Science, I had an opportunity to discuss possible inclusions with professors of English and history at Duke University and the University of North Carolina: Clarence Gohdes, Jay Hubbell, Lewis Leary, Louis Rubin, Jr., and others. Twenty-five books were chosen, ranging in date from 1624 to 1951. *Books That Changed the South* was published by the UNC Press in 1977, and a paperback edition was produced at the same time by Littlefield, Adams. In general, the book met with a friendly reception by Southern literary critics and historians, though some unreconstructed Confederates disagreed with my verdicts on John C. Calhoun, Frances Kemble, and Frederick Law Olmsted, among others. Some skeptics expressed doubt that any given group of books had actually changed the South, arguing that a region so large and complex was unlikely to have been substantially shaped by books.

Still pursuing my concept that books have played major roles in the advance of civilization, I next branched out into two more specialized areas: travel and science. Travel literature has always held a special appeal for me. My first trip outside the United States was made after my junior year in college. Since then, I have been to thirty-eight countries, scattered among all five inhabited continents, in some instances for extended stays. In 1978, the ALA published *In Search of New Horizons, Epic Tales of Travel and Exploration,* in many ways my favorite among all the books that I have written. I am convinced that travel narratives have frequently had decisive impacts on historical events, such as encouraging further explorations, stimulating the colonization and settlement of new lands, and broadening man's view of his world. *In Search of New Horizons* includes twenty-four books based on the great explorers' own accounts, beginning with Herodotus in the fifth century B.C. and ending with Edmund Hillary's conquest of Mt. Everest in 1953. Only one chapter drew any adverse comment. One reviewer cast doubt on whether the North Pole had actually been reached by Robert Peary, though most historians credit him with that feat.

In preparation for writing *In Search of New Horizons,* I read the classic narratives of travel by Marco Polo, Magellan, Vespucci, James Cook, Mungo Park, Alexander von Humboldt, Lewis and Clark, Francis Parkman, Charles Darwin, Richard Henry Dana, Richard Burton, Henry Stanley, Joshua Slocum, Theodore Roosevelt, Thor Heyerdahl, Maurice Herzog, Roald Amundsen, and other pioneers.

A recent work, *Landmarks in Science, Hippocrates to Carson,* published by Libraries Unlimited in 1982, takes a broad view of scientific development. Included are seventy-six works which I believe have most influenced scientific history from the ancient to the modern world. Lawrence Thompson, writing in *American Notes and Queries,* concluded, "This work could be used as a textbook in any course on the history of science. From Aristotle, Theophrastus, and Euclid, through Avicenna, Leonardo and Copernicus, up to Freud, the Curies, Kinsey, and Einstein, there is a lucid account of basic scientific research in the Occident, touching all major detail."

Another offshoot of my preoccupation with books drew me into some biographical writing. Dr. Samuel Smith, with whom I had worked when he was editor for Barnes & Noble, had gone on to serve as editor for "Twayne's Great Educators Series." I contracted, at Dr. Smith's invitation, to write the lives of four great educational leaders. These were published over a five-year period, from 1974 to 1978: *Horace Mann, Champion of Public Schools, Heinrich Pestalozzi, Father of Modern Pedagogy, Henry Barnard,* and *Friedrich Froebel.*

Some of the information from my writings on the influence of books was adapted for *Memorable Americans, 1750–1950,* written jointly with John T. Flanagan and Harold W. Scott, published by Libraries Unlimited in 1983.

An opportunity to recapitulate and reassess my conclusions relating to the influence of books came in 1973, when the Illinois Library School faculty invited me to present the Windsor Lectures for that year. The series of lectures, published the following year under the title *Books and History,* developed four main themes: first, the genesis of certain great scientific concepts; second, an attempt to reappraise certain historical reputations; third, the impact of books on American history; and fourth, "The Great American Success Story," noting the constant emphasis on material success by such popular writers as Benjamin Franklin, Horatio Alger, Dale Carnegie, and others, though many of the most admired characters in American history never attained great wealth. *Books and History* was translated into Spanish, with the title *Libros e Historia,* by Victor Manuel de Las Casas, and published in Panama in 1982.

In reading the variety of books, numbering several hundred, that I have discussed in my studies of influential works, two main considerations have guided me. First, they had to meet the criterion of historical significance, that is, there had to be convincing evidence of their impact on the world at large or in some specific sphere of activity. In the second place, I was swayed by my subjective reactions toward the books and their authors. In most instances, I found the books intellectually stimulating—an essential quality. Beyond that point, however, I was often deeply stirred by the books' messages, a factor that must have contributed vastly to their influence. Examples are Thomas Paine's impassioned pleading for independence in *Common Sense;* Thoreau's resistance to tyrannical government; the fight of great scientists such as Roger Bacon, Galileo, and Vesalius for scientific truth at the risk of their lives; the inspiring discoveries of Charles Darwin's voyage with the H.M.S. *Beagle;* the courageous defense of the rights of women by Mary Wollstonecraft; the exposure of the evils of slavery by Stowe; and many others.

Naturally, I have been curious about attempts made by other critics to identify and assess the influence of books. There have been a number of such efforts. Edmund Weeks, John Dewey, and Charles Beard in 1935 drew up a list of fifty titles they believed had made the greatest impact, but only three were unanimous choices (Karl Marx's *Das Kapital*, Edward Bellamy's *Looking Backward*, and James Frazer's *The Golden Bough*). A few years later (1939), Malcolm Cowley and Bernard Smith used a similar approach in *Books That Changed Our Minds*. One hundred thirty-four titles were recommended by experts in various fields, from which Cowley and Smith selected only twelve. In 1945, an English writer, Horace Shipp, published the small volume *Books That Moved the World*, confining his list to ten works from ancient to modern times. A Princeton historian, Eric F. Goldman, published an article in the *Saturday Review* in 1953 entitled "Books That Changed America." In the end, his list was limited to fifteen books, some of which now seem considerably dated.

It is a game still being played. The National Council of Teachers of English published *Books I Read When I Was Young: The Favorite Books of Famous People* (1980). The Sabines' interviews with individuals in 43 states engaged in 144 different occupations resulted in *Books That Made the Difference* (1983). They listed 167 titles by more than 150 authors named by interviewees. In each case, the person's choice was explained and defended. Altogether, the Sabine study presents a remarkable view of the reading interests and habits, often totally unexpected, of a great variety of Americans.

Also in 1983, Edwin Castagna, retired director of the Enoch Pratt Library in Baltimore, published *Caught in the Act: The Decisive Reading of Some Notable Men and Women and Its Influence on Their Actions and Attitudes*. Castagna cites my *Books That Changed the World* and *Books That Changed America*, as well as Waples, Berelson, and Bradshaw's *What Reading Does to People*, Cowley and Smith's *Books That Changed Our Minds*, and Frances Walsh's *First Discoveries in the Magic World of Books*.

The American literary historian Jay B. Hubbell in *Who Are the Major American Writers?* (1972) analyzes a number of efforts to resolve the question. His chapter on "The Most Influential Books" is mainly concerned with the ways in which specific books have affected society in general, rather than with their impact on individuals. Hubbell concludes, "It would appear that it is almost as difficult to select the most influential books as it is to name those that eventually will be recognized as literary masterpieces." Hubbell offers several criticisms of *Books That Changed the World,* but decides that "Downs, however, it seems to me performed his task more successfully than Goldman, Cowley and Smith, or Horace Shipp."

Castagna's approach, assessing how specific individuals have been influenced by their reading, has merit. It required extensive reading of biographies and autobiographies. Unquestionably, the impact of books on important people is significant. It may be doubted, however, whether the influence on individuals is as meaningful as are changes that affect society in general. Also, it may reasonably be asked, in view of the readability difficulty of many highly important works, whether those books could have exerted influence on any except a narrow band of specialists. Certainly few laymen could comprehend and follow with ease the original Latin texts of Copernicus, Harvey, and Newton, or Einstein's theories in any language. Only the trained social scientist may appreciate fully the often tortuous reasoning of an Adam Smith, a Malthus, or a Marx; while a biological background enriches one's understanding of a Vesalius, a Darwin, or a Freud.

The answer to the question is that most people obtain ideas secondhand, predigested, by way of a filtering-down process through such media as popularizations in book form, magazines and newspapers, classroom lessons, public lectures, and more recently, radio, television, and motion pictures. The influence of very technical works, accordingly, has usually resulted from interpretations by experts. Applications to daily living are made without the conscious knowledge of people generally, as for example, the mechanistic discoveries of Newton or Einstein's theories in relation to nuclear fission and atomic energy.

A frequent weakness of most attempts to list the most influential books is a lack of perspective. The compilers are too near recently published works to make valid historical judgments. A new book that seems significant today may be outmoded and outdated a decade hence. A perspective of between twenty-five and fifty years may therefore be needed before a book's influence and long-range importance can be fully evaluated.

❄ ❄ ❄

Throughout a forty-year career as a university librarian, one of my prime objects was to build great research collections. For me, there is an excitement, a fascination, and a satisfaction about developing collections for a major research library unequaled by any other aspect of librarianship. Because the world of books covers the universe, its full exploitation demands the most erudite scholarship, close collaboration among many people with diverse knowledge and interests, familiarity with the publishing industry and the book trade, and generous financial support. It has been my good fortune to have been directly associated with the growth of three leading American university libraries whose collections have expanded into millions of volumes. At the same time, it has been gratifying to note a steady increase in the rate of book publishing and in the circulation of books in public libraries.

Aside from reading for professional purposes, I have always had an active personal involvement with books. For the past fifty years, I have been an assiduous collector of American humor and folklore, originally inspired perhaps by my origin in an area rich in folk tales and folk songs: western North Carolina. For recreational reading, I am a devotee of the detective story (among my favorites: Sherlock Holmes, S.S. Van Dine, James M. Cain, and Agatha Christie), accounts of travel in remote corners of the world (from Herodotus and Marco Polo to Lowell Thomas, Harry Franck, Richard Halliburton, Vilhjalmur Stefansson, and Alan Moorehead), and political satire (notably "Mr. Dooley," H.L. Mencken, Will Rogers, and Art Buchwald).

And so my lifelong love affair with books and reading continues, unaffected by automation, computers, and all other forms of twentieth-century gadgetry.

TYPE
Meridien 54

COMPOSITION
Carver Photocomposition, Inc.

COVER PAPER
Curtis Tweedweave, brown

TEXT PAPER
Mohawk Superfine Softwhite

PRINTING
Printing Incorporated

DESIGN
Stephen Kraft

FOIL STAMPING
Raff Embossing